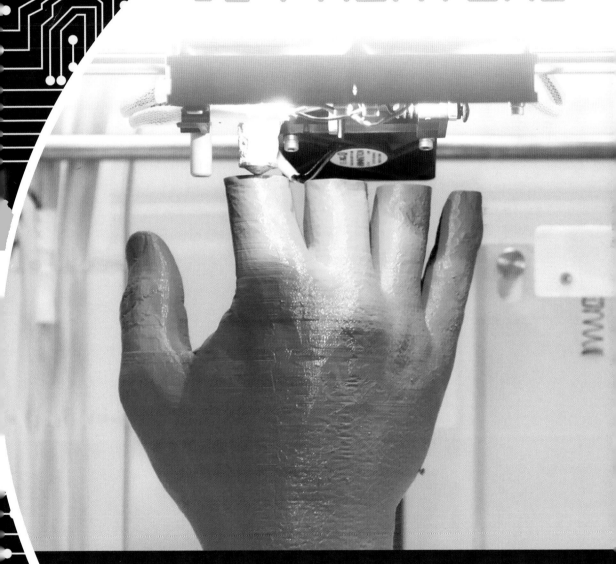

3D PRINTERS

BY YVETTE LaPIERRE

CONTENT CONSULTANT
Howard A. Kuhn, PhD
Adjunct Professor, University of Pittsburgh
Technical Advisor, America Makes

Core Library

Cover image: A 3D printer makes a model of a human
hand by printing material layer by layer.

An Imprint of Abdo Publishing
abdobooks.com

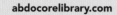

abdocorelibrary.com

Published by Abdo Publishing, a division of ABDO, PO Box 398166, Minneapolis, Minnesota 55439. Copyright © 2019 by Abdo Consulting Group, Inc. International copyrights reserved in all countries. No part of this book may be reproduced in any form without written permission from the publisher. Core Library™ is a trademark and logo of Abdo Publishing.

Printed in the United States of America, North Mankato, Minnesota
092018
012019

Cover Photo: iStockphoto
Interior Photos: iStockphoto, 1, 4–5, 8, 22 (middle), 29; Alexander Tolstykh/Shutterstock Images, 6, 43; Monkey Business Images/iStockphoto, 12–13; Shutterstock Images, 15; Francois Nascimbeni/AFP/Getty Images, 18–19; Moreno Soppelsa/Shutterstock Images, 22 (top); Mrina Skoropadskaya/iStockphoto, 22 (bottom); Mark Williamson/Science Source, 23; Richard Levine/Corbis/Getty Images, 26–27; Guo Jianjun/Imaginechina/AP Images, 31; Maxim Grigoryev/TASS/Getty Images, 32–33, 45; Robert Clark/National Geographic, 37; NASA, 39

Editor: Megan Ellis
Series Designer: Ryan Gale

Library of Congress Control Number: 2018949769

Publisher's Cataloging-in-Publication Data

Names: LaPierre, Yvette, author.
Title: Inside 3D printers / by Yvette LaPierre.
Description: Minneapolis, Minnesota : Abdo Publishing, 2019 | Series: Inside technology | Includes online resources and index.
Identifiers: ISBN 9781532117886 (lib. bdg.) | ISBN 9781641856133 (pbk) | ISBN 9781532170744 (ebook)
Subjects: LCSH: Technological innovations--Juvenile literature. | Three-dimensional printing--Juvenile literature. | Rapid prototyping—Juvenile literature.
Classification: DDC 621.988--dc23

CONTENTS

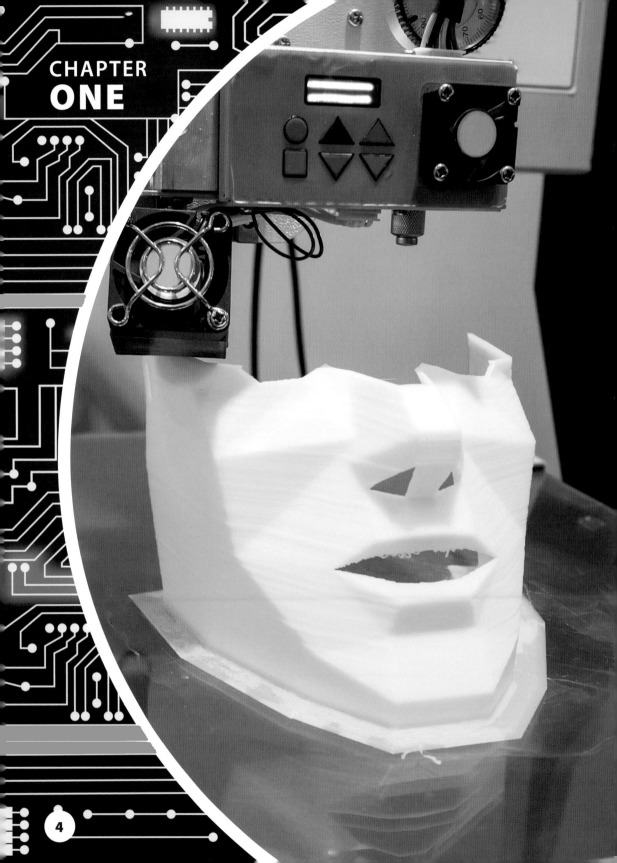

PRINTING IN THREE DIMENSIONS

The print head in the three-dimensional (3D) printer begins to move. Guided by a computer, it traces an outline on the printer bed. Liquid plastic comes out of the nozzle in the print head. It creates a curved line on the printer bed. The nozzle lifts slightly and moves back and forth. It lays down another layer on top of the first one. It squirts layer after layer. The plastic cools and hardens as the printed object builds upward. A pattern begins to appear.

3D printers can print models of many things, such as famous landmarks and human faces.

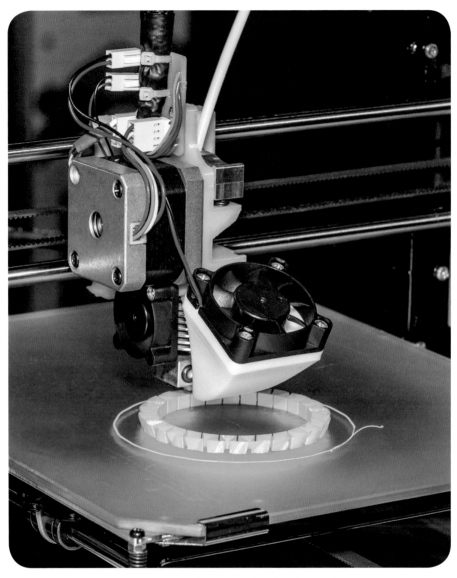

3D printers can use materials to make hollow objects.

The printer works for many hours. Then, the computer tells the printer to stop. A model of a human face sits on the printer bed.

A 3D printer is similar to an inkjet printer, which many people use at home, school, and work. Inkjet printers deposit ink on flat pieces of paper. This is printing in two dimensions (2D). A 3D printer deposits material, too. But it builds objects in three dimensions. You can hold the printed object in your hand.

A 3D printer does not use ink. It uses plastic, metal, or other materials. The technical name for 3D printing is additive manufacturing (AM). That's because 3D printing makes objects by adding material layer by layer.

ADDING VERSUS SUBTRACTING

AM is a relatively new process. The traditional way to make things is subtractive manufacturing. Material is removed from an object until the desired shape appears. This may involve sawing, grinding, or carving. It creates a lot of waste. AM builds the object in the desired shape. It produces little or no waste. That can make AM less expensive and better for the environment.

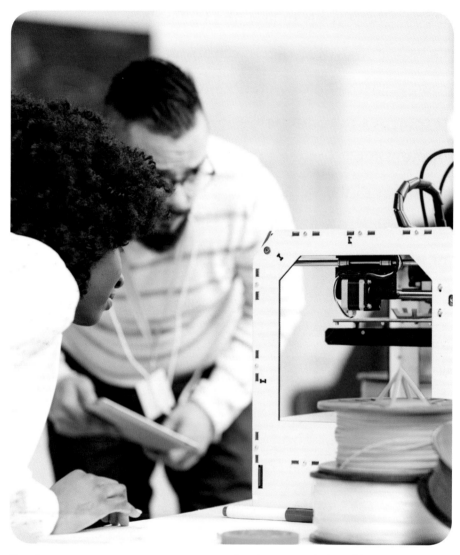

Engineers can use prototypes to look at models of larger objects that they want to create.

RAPID PROTOTYPES

Engineers developed 3D printing in the 1980s and

early 1990s. At first, 3D printing was used to quickly

create prototypes. In fact, the technology was originally called rapid prototyping. A prototype is similar to a rough draft of an object. Engineers and designers use prototypes to test their designs. They can make sure all of the pieces work correctly before creating thousands of copies of the object. Prototypes can be made in hours using 3D printing. Before that, it could take days or even longer to make them by hand.

The first 3D printers made objects that weren't very strong. They did not last a long time. They were only temporary. Then engineers began to develop ways to print better materials. Now 3D printers can make machine parts and much more.

3D PRINTERS AT WORK

Most 3D printers are industrial. This means they are used in factories. They print parts for machines such as trucks and airplanes. These printers can print an object as large as a car or as small as the head of a pin.

BUILDING A BEAK

A bald eagle named Beauty was shot in the face by a poacher. The eagle survived. But much of her beak was gone. An eagle needs a beak to eat and groom its feathers. A bird specialist and an engineer came to her rescue. They designed a prosthetic beak for Beauty. They printed it on a 3D printer. Beauty now lives at the Birds of Prey Northwest rescue. She uses her new beak to eat her favorite food: strips of salmon.

3D printers are also great for making items that are hard to find. For example, an owner of an antique car can print a part that is no longer available. Aerospace companies can print custom parts for a single rocket.

Medical and dental supply businesses also use 3D printers. They print items such as braces, contact lenses, and hearing aids. These items are designed and printed to fit each individual patient. 3D printers can also print prostheses. These are artificial body parts such as arms and legs. People who are missing a limb often use prostheses. 3D printers can make a prosthetic device that fits the person's body perfectly.

Artists and designers can create beautiful items with 3D printers. They can print jewelry, sculptures, and clothes. 3D printing technology is progressing rapidly. Advances in software and hardware mean new materials can be used. New materials will allow for new uses. In the future, 3D printers may appear in most businesses and homes. They may even work on Mars one day.

EXPLORE ONLINE

Chapter One gives a basic description of how 3D printing works. The website below shows the 3D printing of a whale fossil. How does it help you better understand how 3D printers create objects?

3D-PRINTED WHALE FOSSIL
abdocorelibrary.com/inside-3D-printers

CHAPTER
TWO

DESIGN SOFTWARE

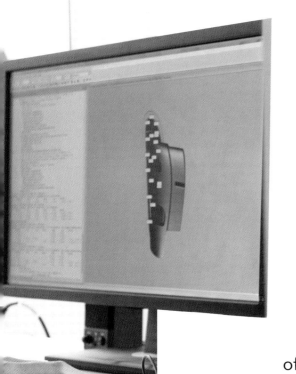

Before a 3D printer makes an object, engineers or designers create the design using computers and design software. They save the design into a design file. A design file is an electronic picture of the object to be printed. It is like a blueprint that guides a builder.

The design describes the shape of the object in three dimensions. It describes the object's height, width, and depth. The design also describes all features of the object.

People use computers to create design files for 3D printing.

These features might include holes and curves. The computer with the design file connects to a 3D printer. The design file tells the 3D printer what it needs to print and which materials to use.

COMPUTER-AIDED DESIGN SOFTWARE

Designers use computer-aided design (CAD) software programs. CAD programs allow designers to draw on a computer screen instead of paper. A drawing on paper shows the object in two dimensions. A CAD design shows the object in three dimensions. Designers can look at the object from any side or angle. Keyboard commands and mouse movements can flip

3D SCANS

Engineers can scan an existing object or shape using lasers to create a 3D design. This involves shooting thousands of dots of light at the object. A scanner device records every dot. Then the dots are loaded into a computer. The computer organizes them. It connects the dots to each other. Then it fills in holes. Finally, the dots create a 3D version of the original object.

DESIGN
COORDINATES

A design file maps every point of an object to a location in space along X, Y, and Z. Y is front to back. X is side to side. Z is up and down. Each printed layer is one layer up in the Z direction. When put together, X, Y, and Z show a coordinate. A coordinate is the location of something. It is usually represented as (X, Y, Z). A 3D shape can have millions of coordinates. Look at the diagram below. How do these coordinates tell the 3D printer what shapes to print?

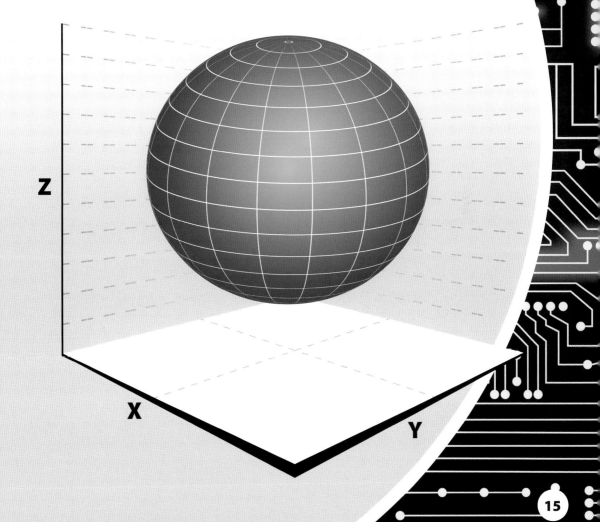

AMATEUR DESIGNERS

CAD software takes a lot of training to use. But amateurs are finding ways to use design files with home and office 3D printers. 3D printing apps allow users who don't know CAD to design objects. People can build simple objects such as smartphone cases.

Another option is to use someone else's 3D design. Some websites provide free digital designs. These sites include Thingiverse, Yeggi, STL Finder, and GrabCAD. Users can find millions of designs for objects. These objects range from a toy robot to a watch. The National Aeronautic and Space Administration (NASA) even has 3D designs for some of its rockets and satellites. Users can print models of spacecraft such as the Curiosity rover.

or rotate the design. CAD programs assist in the creation of a design. Engineers and designers can use different tools in the software to make an object larger or smaller. They can even change the color of a design before it goes to the printer. Designers can also create the objects quickly. CAD software is much faster than making the models by hand. It is also more accurate.

FROM SOFTWARE TO OBJECT

Software works with the CAD design. It slices the 3D image into thin, flat layers. The flat layers stack up like a stack of playing cards or slices in a loaf of bread. This creates the object.

For each 2D slice, the printer's nozzle deposits material along the outline of the design's shape. Then it fills in the area inside the outline. The printer repeats this process for each slice of the CAD file. That builds the 3D object.

FURTHER EVIDENCE

Chapter Two discusses how designers use CAD software to draw objects for 3D printing. What was one of the main points of the chapter? The website below teaches the basics of CAD design. It also includes examples of designs. Does the information on the site help you understand better how 3D designs are made? Does it give you a better idea of what 3D designs look like? Does it make you want to tinker with 3D designing?

TINKERCAD
abdocorelibrary.com/inside-3D-printers

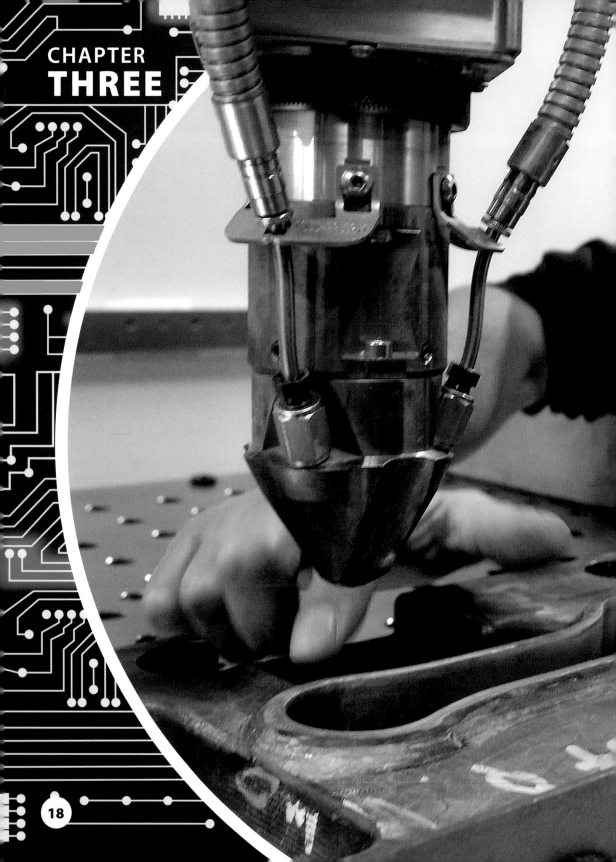

PRINTER HARDWARE

All 3D printers are driven by a design file. The printer connects to a computer that holds the design file. Material with little or no form is fed into the printer. For example, the material might be liquid, paste, or powder. 3D printers turn the raw material into a solid form. The design file determines the shape. The type of material determines the printer hardware.

PRINTER FAMILIES

Engineers have developed different methods for applying different types of raw materials. Experts divide 3D printing technologies into

A 3D printer in Charleville-Mezieres, France, prepares to deposit metal material from its nozzle.

3D SELFIES

Selfies can be posted on the internet, but they can also be printed in 3D. A company called UScan360 makes what it called "3D Selfies." It takes a photo of someone in a 3D capture booth. Then, designers create design files from the picture. A 3D printer, guided by the design file, prints a 3D version of the selfie. The result is a selfie statue. The statues are printed in full color. They can be full bodies or just heads. While not technically selfies, these statues show the possibilities of 3D scanning technology.

two families. The first family of printers has nozzles. They deposit raw material through a nozzle on the print head. The printer builds the object by laying down layer after layer of material.

The second family of printer does not deposit raw material. Instead, it moves a laser over a bed of raw material. The laser follows the design file. This material is usually a powder. The laser turns the powder into a solid. The printer continues this process layer by layer.

STEREOLITHOGRAPHY

Stereolithography (SLA) was the first 3D printing method developed. Engineer Chuck Hull introduced it in the 1980s. SLA uses liquid plastic and a laser beam.

The liquid plastic fills a vat. The design file controls the motion of a laser beam. A laser beam passes over the vat. This hardens one layer of plastic in the shape of the design. The object lowers into the vat by one layer. The laser beam passes over again and again.

SLA is fast. It is accurate. It prints plastic objects with a smooth surface. People use SLA for detailed objects such as dental braces and invisible hearing aids.

FUSED DEPOSITION MODELING

The second method of 3D printing is fused deposition modeling (FDM). It was introduced in 1991. It is used in most desktop 3D printers. The material is a long strand of thin plastic. A spool behind the printer holds the plastic. The printer heats the plastic as it enters the nozzle. It becomes soft and flexible. The nozzle draws

TYPES OF 3D
PRINTERS

This table shows the differences between types of 3D printers. How does the diagram help you understand how 3D printers work? What projects might you want to use each printer for?

	Materials	How It Works	Applications
Stereolithography	Liquid plastic	Laser beam hardens layers of plastic	Detailed objects such as medical equipment
Fused Deposition Modeling	Spools of plastic	Nozzle on the print head puts down layers of plastic	Toys and prototypes
Selective Laser Sintering	Glass and powders of plastic, ceramic, or metal	A roller spreads the powder, which is then fused together by a laser	A variety of objects from custom clothes to models of body parts that are used to plan surgeries

An FDM printer was used to create a model of the NASA Orion spacecraft.

Orion
3D Printed 1/20 Scale
Orion Capsule and
Service Module

the outline of the object's first layer. Then the print head moves back and forth. Plastic fills in the outline.

The plastic hardens. Then, the print head raises slightly. The second layer prints on top. This process repeats. It may take hours or even days until the object is printed.

FDM printers are the easiest to build. They use inexpensive materials. But FDM-printed materials are not very strong. The surfaces are not smooth. FDM is used mostly to make toys and prototypes.

SELECTIVE LASER SINTERING

Selective laser sintering (SLS) was introduced to the market in 1993. It uses powdered plastic, ceramic, or glass and a laser beam. A roller or flat blade spreads the powder in a layer. The laser moves across the layer of powder. It follows the design. The laser fuses the powder together. This process continues layer by layer.

The SLS method prints a variety of objects. These range from custom clothes to medical models. For example, surgeons use SLS-printed models of a patient's body part to help plan a surgery.

3D-PRINTED SPORTS CAR

Scientists at the Oak Ridge National Laboratory (ORNL) 3D printed a sports car called a Shelby Cobra. The scientists used a very large version of an FDM printer. The process is called big area additive manufacturing (BAAM). The car parts were printed separately. Then they were put together. ORNL introduced the Shelby Cobra at a car show in Detroit, Michigan, in 2015. That marked the 50-year anniversary of the Cobra.

STRAIGHT TO THE
SOURCE

Hod Lipson and Melba Kurman wrote the book *Fabricated: The New World of 3D Printing*. In the book, they discuss some of the current uses of 3D printers as well as what 3D printers might be able to do in the future:

> *NASA test-drives a version of its Mars Rover in the Arizona desert. On board the Rover are several custom-made printed metal parts. Many of these parts have complicated shapes made of curves and inner hollows that could not have been manufactured by anything other than a 3D printer. . . .*
>
> *These modest manufacturing miracles are already taking place. In the not-so-distant future, people will 3D print living tissue, nutritionally calibrated food, and ready-made, fully assembled electronic components.*
>
> Source: Hod Lipson and Melba Kurman. *Fabricated: The New World of 3D Printing.* Hoboken, NJ: John Wiley & Sons, 2013. Print. 68.

Back It Up

The author of this passage is using evidence to support a point. Write a paragraph describing the point the author is making. Then write down two or three pieces of evidence the author uses to make the point.

MATERIALS

The first 3D printers used plastic as a material. Plastic is still the most common material used in 3D printers. But new technologies allow 3D printers to handle a variety of materials. Common materials include metals and ceramics. Special printers can print living cells. Printers can even be adapted to print food.

PLASTIC

3D printers use plastics that melt when they are heated. They turn solid when they cool. Most LEGO bricks are made from this type of plastic. Once the plastic sets, it can be sanded smooth. It can be painted. Pigments can also be added to the raw plastic.

A Piecemaker 3D printer kiosk can quickly print plastic toys such as a model of a truck.

Many objects can be printed from plastic. Car companies print plastic prototypes of dashboards and other car parts. Airplanes have 3D-printed plastic parts. They make the plane lighter. Hobbyists print toys, chess pieces, phone cases, and many other plastic items. Artists and designers have printed plastic ornaments, furniture, and even a working electric guitar.

CUSTOM CLOTHES

One material that can't go into a 3D printer is fabric. Fashion designers use plastic instead. It moves and drapes like regular fabric. But it is stiff. However, plastic fabric may be perfect for astronauts. NASA is working on a strong 3D-printed fabric for spacesuits. They want it to protect astronauts in space.

METALS

Researchers have developed methods to 3D-print different metals. These metals include steel, titanium, and even tungsten. One way is to use a selective laser melting (SLM) printer. The printer adds the metal in powder form. A laser beam melts the

metal powder. Then the unfused powder is shaken off. The result is a strong metal object.

3D printers can build metal gears, hinges, and other parts for machines. NASA has printed metal engine parts for rockets. Some people even have 3D-printed knees. They are made from titanium.

CERAMICS

3D printers can print ceramic items, too. The process is similar to FDM. The raw material is ceramic powder.

It is then mixed in a fluid. The mixture comes out of the print head. Then the printed object goes into a furnace. The fluid burns off. The result is a solid ceramic object.

Printed ceramic is smooth and strong. Bone implants can be made from ceramic. They are strong and don't splinter in the body. Ceramic can withstand heat high enough to melt metal. This is why scientists are working on 3D-printed ceramic parts for jet engines.

PIZZA IN SPACE

Sending food into space isn't easy. Fresh food can spoil on a long mission. 3D printers may be the answer to this problem. Astronauts could bring the raw materials such as protein powders to print healthy meals in space. NASA funded a project to print a pizza in space. This technology might be used on future missions to Mars.

FOOD

Some foods can be 3D printed much the same way as any other material. The first step is to create a design file for the shape the food will take. Then the food is loaded into the nozzle. The food must be a soft paste, such

Mooncakes are round Chinese pastries filled with red bean paste. They can be printed on a 3D printer.

as cookie dough. The printer spreads the food in the shape of the design, layer by layer. Candy, chocolates, and pizza have been printed.

THE FUTURE OF 3D PRINTING

Advances in technology are leading to new uses for 3D printing. Design software has become faster and easier to use. New 3D printing methods can use different materials. 3D printing has the potential to change many fields, including architecture, medicine, and even space travel.

FUTURE FOOD

3D printers for food mostly print fancy chocolates and candy now. But someday, every home could have a food printer. The printers might have lasers. The lasers would cook the food as it came out of the printer. This could save time and money.

3D printers could provide food for people who do not have access to fresh food. For example, 3D printers could print food for soldiers in the field or refugees in a camp. They could print personalized food for a person's exact nutritional needs.

PRINTERS THAT THINK

3D printers simply follow directions. The design file tells the printer what to print and where. The printer can't "see" what it is printing. If the design is correct, the printer will print the object. It might be a shoe or a toy frog. But if something goes wrong, the printer might create a lump of plastic. In the future, a 3D printer might be able to watch what it is printing. It could adjust the printing if needed. Researchers are working on 3D printers that can think and fix problems.

3D HOMES

In 2014, a construction company in China printed ten small houses in just one day. Printers created separate parts, including walls and floors. Then the parts were put together.

3D printing is much faster and cheaper than traditional building methods.

The next step is to print an entire building in one continuous process. Engineers are developing two methods to do that. One method is called D-Shape, which uses an enormous 3D printer to print a house out of sand. First the architect designs the home using CAD software. The computer is hooked up to the printer on the building site. The printer sprays a thin layer of sand. Then it sprays a layer of glue. The glue turns the sand into a solid. The entire house is built layer by layer from the bottom up.

ECOFRIENDLY PRINTING

Researchers are experimenting with using recycled materials in 3D printers. Students at the University of Washington made a recycled plastic boat. They used 40 pounds (18 kg) of plastic milk jugs. First, they ground the jugs into a fine powder. Then they fed the powder into a 3D printer. The students spent two days printing the boat. The boat could carry 150 pounds (68 kg).

Another method is called Contour Crafting. It uses a mobile 3D printer on wheels or tracks. The printer travels up the building as it prints. The printer deposits concrete paste out of its nozzle. It traces the footprint of the house. Then it travels higher to lay down the next layer. Each layer hardens. The house grows from the bottom up.

BIOPRINTING

One future of medical 3D printing is bioprinting. Bioprinting uses 3D printing to replace human body parts. Researchers have already printed some body parts. They have printed bone, cartilage, and a trachea. Now they are developing 3D printers to create more complex body parts. They hope to print tissue, organs, and other parts soon. But these parts are harder to print. Blood vessels need to be printed inside the tissue. These vessels are very small.

The first step in bioprinting is to design a computer model of the organ or limb. Then the design file is

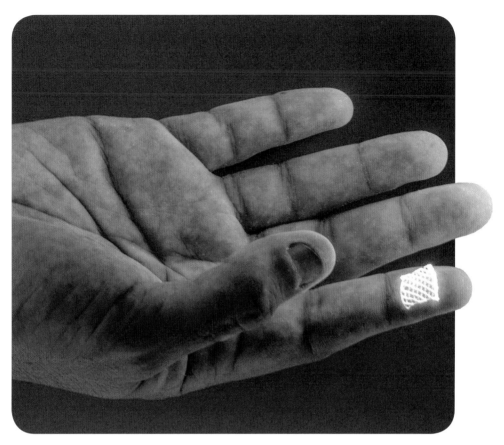

Scientists at Harvard University printed living tissue with blood vessels, seen here under black light. Though bioprinting could replace animal testing, this process remains expensive.

sent to a 3D printer. The material used in bioprinting is similar to a living ink. It is a printable gel that has living cells in it. The gel protects the cells as they squeeze through the printing nozzle. The gel also feeds the cells. It helps them grow. The cell material must be printed quickly to keep its shape. The printer needs several nozzles to print different types of cells at once.

Medical researchers imagine a future when people don't have to wait for transplants. Instead, technicians can print a new kidney, lung, or leg for them. Or a doctor could press a button and print out a sheet of skin for a burn victim.

3D PRINTERS IN SPACE

NASA is developing new technologies to use 3D printers in space. They must work in zero gravity. Liquids do not behave the same in space as they do on Earth. Material does not flow or bond the same. This can result in a weaker object. Researchers are working to solve these problems. When they do, space printers could have many uses.

In the future, NASA may establish bases on the moon or Mars. 3D printers could help astronauts

In 2014, a 3D printer on the International Space Station printed a ratchet wrench. Researchers are working on other ways that 3D printers can be used in space.

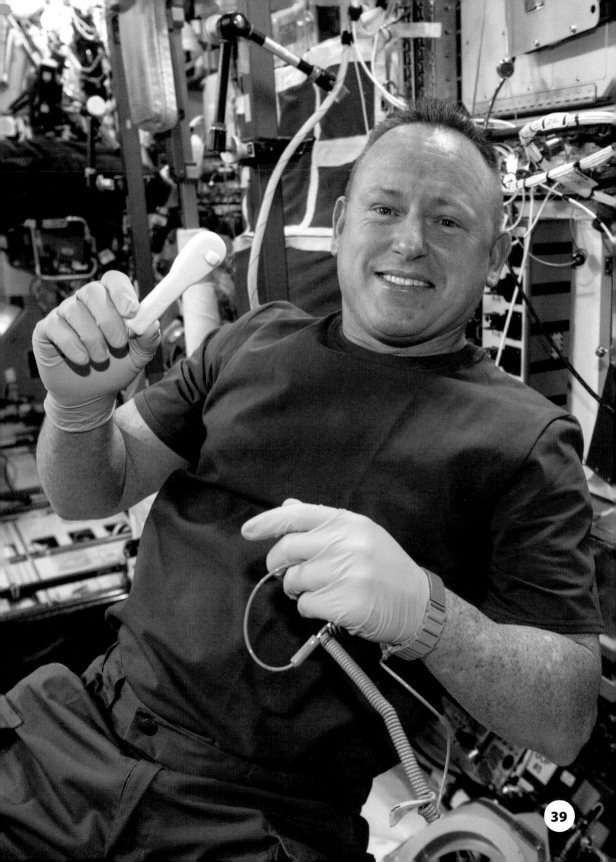

live on these bases for a long time. They could print replacement parts or tools they need. They might even print entire machines. 3D printers might be able to use raw materials found on the moon or Mars. The materials might be used to print buildings. Bioprinters could print fresh meat and vegetables. Or they could print body parts for sick or injured astronauts.

3D printers and their products are already all around us. In the near future, people may ride 3D-printed bikes to 3D-printed schools or malls. New technologies, software, and materials are opening up a world of possibilities for 3D printers.

STRAIGHT TO THE
SOURCE

Author Elizabeth Royte believes that the growth of the 3D printer business has some legal and security risks. In an article for the *Smithsonian*, she writes:

> *Who is liable if a home-printed design fails to perform? Who owns the intellectual property of codes and the objects they produce? . . . . Disney, whose characters are widely copied by [people who use 3D printers], is so far ignoring infringements, but that may change.*
>
> *Then there are security concerns. Using blueprints downloaded from the internet, people already have begun printing gun parts. Hackers have stolen personal banking information after creating a widget that fits inside an ATM. . . . Tools can be used for good as easily as for ill.*

Source: Elizabeth Royte. "What Lies Ahead for 3-D Printing." *Smithsonian.com.* Smithsonian, May 2013. Web. Accessed May 11, 2018.

Changing Minds

Imagine you have to convince your best friend about the possible dangers of 3D printing. How would you convince your friend? Make sure you explain your opinion. Include facts and details that support your reasons.

FAST FACTS

- 3D printing was developed in the 1980s. It was a way to make prototypes quickly and inexpensively.

- 3D printing is also known as additive manufacturing.

- 3D printers build objects layer by layer.

- Design files are created using CAD software. The design file tells the printer what to print and where using coordinates. These are often written (X, Y, Z). The layers make up the Z axis. The Y axis is front to back. The X axis is side to side.

- 3D printers are primarily industrial and used in manufacturing.

- 3D printers can use plastic, metal, ceramic, concrete, and other materials.

- NASA is developing new technologies to use 3D printers in space. Buildings, tools, and food may be printed for astronauts on future space missions.

- Bioprinting is the process of 3D printing replacement body parts. Some body parts have already been printed, but researchers are working on ways to print more complex body parts.

- Researchers are experimenting with using recycled materials in 3D printers.

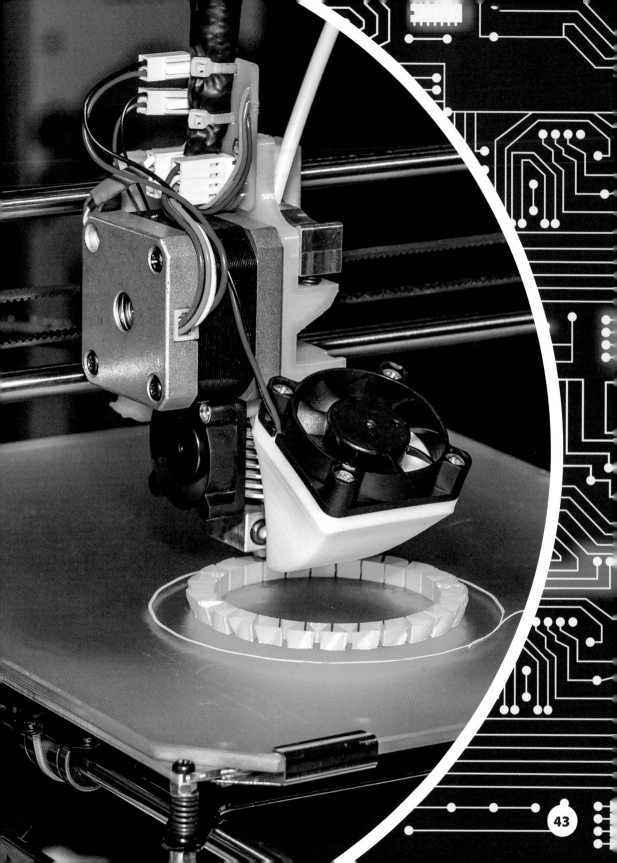

STOP AND
THINK

Tell the Tale
This book describes various things that are made with 3D printers. Imagine you have a 3D printer. What would you print and why? Write 200 words about your design.

Dig Deeper
After reading this book, what questions do you still have about 3D printing? With an adult's help, find a few reliable sources that can help you answer your questions. Write a paragraph about what you learned.

Why Do I Care?
You may not have a 3D printer in your home or school. But that doesn't mean you can't think about ways 3D printers might impact your life. Have you ever seen or used a 3D-printed object? Have any of your friends or family done so? Can you imagine ways you might use 3D-printed objects in the future?

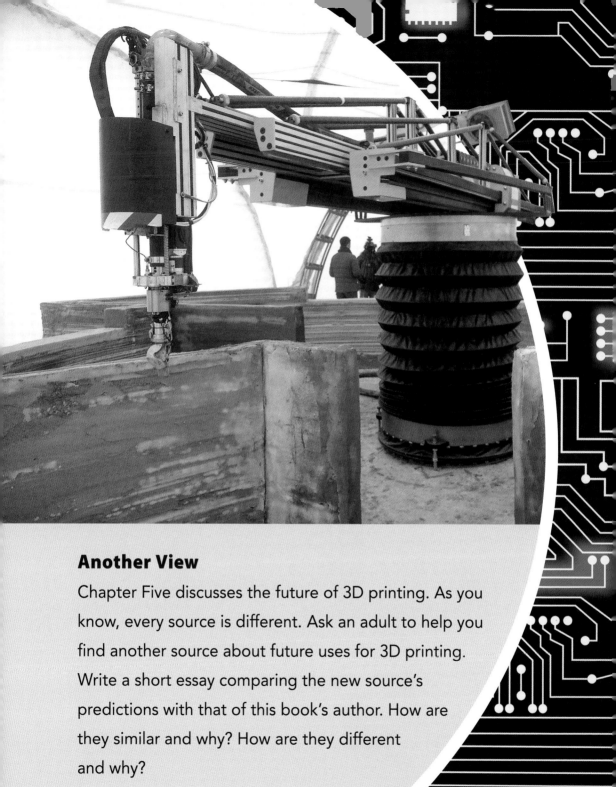

Another View

Chapter Five discusses the future of 3D printing. As you know, every source is different. Ask an adult to help you find another source about future uses for 3D printing. Write a short essay comparing the new source's predictions with that of this book's author. How are they similar and why? How are they different and why?

GLOSSARY

architecture
the process of designing and drawing plans for a building

cartilage
a strong, elastic tissue found in the outer ear, nose, and other places in the body

industrial
something that deals with business and manufacturing

laser
a device that produces an intense narrow beam of light

pigments
things that give color to other materials

satellites
manufactured objects put in orbit to collect information or for communication

three-dimensional (3D)
having the three dimensions of length, width, and height

titanium
a strong but light metal that is very durable

trachea
a tube in humans and other animals that carries air to and from the lungs

tungsten
a rare hard metal that has a very high melting point

two dimensions
the dimensions of length and width but not height

ONLINE RESOURCES

To learn more about 3D printers, visit our free resource websites below.

Core Library
CONNECTION
FREE! COMMON CORE MULTIMEDIA RESOURCES

Visit **abdocorelibrary.com** for free Common Core resources for teachers and students, including vetted activities, multimedia, and booklinks, for deeper subject comprehension.

Booklinks
NONFICTION NETWORK
FREE! ONLINE NONFICTION RESOURCES

Visit **abdobooklinks.com** for free additional online weblinks for further learning. These links are routinely monitored and updated to provide the most current information available.

LEARN MORE

3D Printing Projects. New York: DK Publishing, 2017.

Marquardt, Meg. *Bioengineering in the Real World*. Minneapolis, MN: Abdo, 2016.

INDEX

About the Author

Yvette LaPierre lives in North Dakota with her family, two dogs, and two crested geckos. She writes and edits books and articles for children and adults.